The Beginner's Guide to Coarse Fishing

PAUL DUFFIELD

DEDICATION

This book is dedicated to my son Harry whose enthusiasm for fishing was my inspiration for writing this beginner's guide.

CONTENTS

ACKNOWLEDGMENTS

Images of Coarse Fish
Images of coarse fish used in this guide are reproduced with the kind
permission of the University of Washington Fisheries-Oceanography
Library:
www.lib.washington.edu/about/collections.html

Image of Fishing Reel
Original photo by Jan Tik:
http://www.flickr.com/people/jantik/
Vectorized version by Chabacano:
http://commons.wikimedia.org/wiki/User:Chabacano, licensed under the
Creative Commons Attribution ShareAlike 2.5, Attribution ShareAlike 2.0
and Attribution ShareAlike 1.0 License.

Image Anatomy of a Fish Hook
Image by Mike Cline:
http://commons.wikimedia.org/wiki/User:Mike_Cline, licensed under the
Creative Commons Attribution ShareAlike 3.0, Attribution ShareAlike 2.5,
Attribution ShareAlike 2.0 and Attribution ShareAlike 1.0 License.

Cover Image European Perch
Image by Lauri Rantala from Espoo:
http://www.flickr.com/people/36514345@N00, licensed under the
Creative Commons Attribution 2.0 Generic license.

1 INTRODUCTION

Coarse Fishing, or Coarse Angling to use a more accurate term, is the practice of using a rod and line to catch 'freshwater fish', i.e. fish that live in ponds, lakes, rivers, streams and canals that are not regarded as 'Game Fish'. For practical purposes, this means any fish that does not live in the sea, apart from Salmon and Trout.

There are many so called branches of coarse angling, and you have probably come across terms like Match Angler' and 'Specimen Angler'. These terms are generally used to differentiate Anglers who fish competitively and measure success by the total weight of fish they catch, irrespective of size or species, compared to Anglers who target 'specimen' or large fish, sometimes of one species alone.

In fact, some Anglers specialise in catching just one species, hence the terms 'Carp Angler', 'Pike Angler', 'Barbel Angler' and so on, each 'branch' having its own specialist groups and clubs made up of other Anglers of similar interest.

These days it is possible to go straight into one or other 'branch' of Angling, and be quite successful, if only for a time, by buying pre-made tackle, and following precise instructions on where, how and when to fish. This type of 'instant angling', while it may be enjoyable for a time, rarely leads to a lifelong hobby, its participants drifting away from angling, either because they think they have learned all there is to learn, and done all there is to do, or after a run of unsuccessful fishing trips when the 'instructions' hadn't worked, and they had no 'backup plan'.

A good way to develop angling as a lifelong hobby or interest is to be an 'All Rounder', an Angler who fishes many different waters and styles to catch a variety of different species of fish.

Apart from the obvious fact that they all catch fish, the one thing that Anglers who are successful over the long term in any branch of Angling have in common is that they have a solid grounding in the Angling craft. While they may have found that they prefer one branch of fishing over others, they are quite capable of catching fish in a variety of different circumstances. They can do this because they can call on a storehouse of knowledge built up over a long period of time. In this sense, although they may specialise on one type of fishing or one species of fish, they are 'All Rounders' by background and experience.

The intention of this guide is to give you the basic information you need to be an 'All Rounder' by covering many different styles of fishing for a wide variety of fish in different types of waters.

2 LICENSES AND PERMISSION TO FISH

Anyone aged 12 or over must have a fishing licence to fish for coarse fish. The penalty for being caught fishing without a licence is a fine of up to £2,500.

Full details of current prices can be obtained from the Environment Agency website, where you can also apply for a licence. Licences can also be obtained at post offices.

A licence only allows you to fish legally, it does not mean you can fish anywhere you choose. There are some locations where you can fish for free, but most fishing waters are either owned by fishing clubs that you have to join, or available to fish by purchasing a day ticket.
When you can fish

On rivers there is an annual close season for coarse fishing from 15 March to 15 June each year and you are not allowed to fish using coarse fishing methods during that period.

There is no close season for coarse fishing on lakes, canals and ponds so you are legally allowed to fish all year round, but some clubs enforce their own close season, so check the rules for your chosen fishery before setting out.

If you intend to fish at night, which can be a very productive time for many species, check with your local club or fishery to find out if this is allowed, and whether you need to obtain a special night fishing permit.

3 FISHING TACKLE

All Anglers need 'Tackle', the term used to collectively describe all of the equipment used to catch fish.

Years ago, before modern manufacturing methods allowed specialist items of tackle to be made inexpensively for very specific uses, fishing tackle was made to cover a wide range of fishing situations and only a short section of this guide would have been needed to cover most of the fishing tackle you could buy.

The challenge, today, is to recommend a starter kit that will cover most angling situations without suggesting that you buy ten rods, five reels and a wide assortment of other equipment that it would be impossible to carry to the bank. Indeed, if I was to suggest that you buy the 'specialist' equipment that is available for all of the branches of fishing, so that you always had the tackle that was specifically designed for that type of fishing alone, I would be asking you to spend many thousands of pounds.

To keep things simple, and to keep your outlay on your first fishing kit to a reasonable budget, I will be 'going back to basics' and recommending a range of tackle items that will cover most fishing situations. As your angling career develops you may find that the waters you fish, or the type of fishing you prefer, naturally suggest the purchase of more specialised tackle, but if you equip yourself with the items described in this section, you will have all you need to begin catching most species of fish in most fishing situations.

If you are lucky enough to have a well stocked fishing tackle shop near where you live, after reading this guide you can go there and look at the various items available. If not, there are a lot of online retailers of fishing tackle, but the simplest way to find everything you need is on eBay. Many of the larger online retailers have eBay shops, as well as a lot of specialised smaller retailers, so you're sure to find everything you need, and you can compare prices side by side to make sure you get the best deal.

Fishing Rods

There are many fishing rods to choose from. In this section I will give some recommendations for rods suitable for the fishing situations a beginner to coarse fishing will encounter.

Float Fishing Rods

To cover a wide range of float fishing situations I suggest that you buy a general purpose float fishing rod of about 12 feet (3.6 metres) in length. If you are small of stature, or are buying equipment for a child, one of about 10 feet (3 meters) may be a better choice to start with as it will be more manageable.

There is a wide range of affordable float rods, and any rod of this length described as either a 'Float Rod' or 'Match Rod' in a price range between £15 and £20 should be suitable. Avoid telescopic rods and specialist rods designed for short range Carp Fishing, sometimes described as 'Stalking Rods' as these are not versatile enough to cover a wide range of fishing situations.

When considering the purchase of a float rod, take particular care to ensure that it is made of 'Carbon' or 'Carbon Composite' sometimes referred to just as 'Composite'. These rods should be light enough to hold for long periods, whereas cheaper rods made of 'Fibreglass' or described as of 'Glass' construction will be heavier and are much harder to learn to fish with.

Leger Fishing Rods

For legering you will usually be able to manage with a shorter rod than needed for float fishing, and I would suggest a rod of between 8.5 feet (2.6 meters) and 10 feet (3 metres) with a range of push in quivertips. Don't worry about what 'quivertips' are for now, I will explain these in the section on techniques later.

Suitable rods will be described as 'Leger Rods', Quivertip rods' or 'Tip rods' and one costing between £15 and £20 should be suitable for a wide range of leger fishing situations. Very good rods of both 'Carbon' and 'Carbon Composite' material are available at reasonable prices but. leger rods are not held for long periods of time, so a 'Fibreglass' or 'Glass' rod whilst being heavier, will be fine if your budget is restricted.

Poles and Whips

Pole fishing is a method of fishing that does not involve a reel, using a longer 'rod' to which the line is attached to the end. Whip fishing is similar, but with a shorter 'rod' and is a method for catching small fish close to the bank.

It is not necessary to own a Pole or a Whip to catch fish, a float rod will catch fish in the conditions that a Pole or a Whip will, but as Whips can be obtained very cheaply, and Whip fishing is a very easy and enjoyable method of catching small fish that are close to the bank, if your budget will stretch to it, you can buy a whip of about 4 or 5 metres for £5 or less.

If you are planning to teach a child to fish, whip fishing is fishing at its simplest, and is a good way to obtain all you need for a fishing trip for a total outlay of £10 or so.

Rods for Larger Fish

If you intend to try your hand at catching larger fish such as Pike, Carp or large river Barbel, you will need a stronger rod than described earlier.

Although there are specialist rods for each of these species, you can certainly catch Pike on a Carp rod and Carp on a Pike rod, and a rod suitable for either of these species will be suitable for legering the larger rivers for Barbel.

A good compromise that will be suitable for all three species will be described as a 'specialist' or 'big fish' rod, and will be described as having a 'test curve', a technical term used to describe the amount of weight required to bend the rod through 90 degrees.

A rod of 12 feet (3.6 metres) with a test curve of about 1.75 to 2lb will cover most situations when fishing for these larger specimens, including 'Spinning', a general term used for predator fishing with artificial baits for predators such as Pike.

Fishing Reels

As with rods, it is possible to manage with only one reel, but if you do, I suggest that you get one with a spare spool so you can load it with different strengths of line.

There are different types of reel, but for a beginner a reel of the 'Fixed Spool' type is best. Perfectly good fixed spool reels can be bought for about £5 or £6, and if you can afford it, I suggest that you buy two, preferably with a spare spool each.

You will see reels described as being for 'match fishing', 'legering', 'carp fishing' and so on, but any fixed spool reel in the price range above will be perfectly adequate to start with. You will probably find it easier to begin with if you buy two identical reels, and as this means the spools containing the line will be interchangeable, you will have more options too.

Parts of a fishing reel

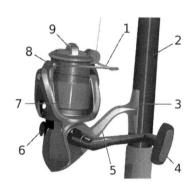

1: Pick up or bail
2: Reel seat
3: Reel foot
4: Handle
5: Support arm
6: Anti-reverse lever
7: Skirted spool
8: Fishing line
9: Drag/clutch adjustment knob

Fishing Nets

There are two types of nets used by Coarse Anglers; Landing Nets and Keep Nets.

Landing Nets

A landing net should be regarded as a necessity as any fish over a few ounces in weight will be difficult to land without one.

There are many sizes and types of landing net, but when you are starting out, pretty much any landing net of about 24 inches (60cm) measured across the widest part will be suitable, with a handle of about 8 feet (2.5 metres).

Check the rules of the waters you intend to fish before buying a net, as some will insist that you have a landing net of at least a minimum size before you are allowed to fish for Carp or Pike. If you are intending to fish such waters, you will need to obtain two landing nets as the larger nets for Carp and Pike fishing are not suitable for general coarse fishing.

You can usually buy nets and handles together for £10 or less, and an alternative to the type with a removable handle is the 'flip up' type of net used by Game Anglers which are perfectly usable for coarse fishing, but make sure you get one with a long enough handle as many of these have short handles designed for use when wading and will not be suitable if you need to fish from a high bank above the water.

Keep Nets

A keep net is used to retain fish in the water until you have finished fishing and is optional, only being required if you are intending to fish competitions, or want to be able to look at the fish you have caught at the end of a session. Many commercial fisheries do not allow the use of keep nets, and may restrict their use for larger fish such as carp.

If you do decide to buy a keep net, make sure it is at least 8 feet (2.5 metres) long and complies with the rules set by the Environment Agency and any waters you intend to fish.

Fishing Line

You will need line for your reels and also for constructing hook lengths. Hook lengths will be explained later in this guide in the section on fishing techniques.

Line for reels

Depending on how many reels and spools you buy, you can load your reels with a range of line strengths. Line choice depends on the conditions and the size and type of fish you expect to catch in a given situation, so carrying a selection is advisable.

If you only have two spools a line of 3lbs (1.4 kg) is suitable for a wide range of float fishing situations, and one of 5lbs (2.3 kg) is suitable for most legering situations.

If you have more than two spools, I would suggest you also load one with line of about 10lbs (4.5 kg) and another with line of 4lb (1.6 kg) or 6lb(2.7 kg) if you are mainly intending to use general fishing techniques to catch a range of fish, or 15lb ((6.8 kg) if you are intending to fish where there are very large specimens of Carp or Pike.

We will cover the different strengths of line used in different angling situations and how to load line on to a reel later in this guide.

There are many manufacturers of line, and the price can vary widely, but inexpensive line is fine to begin with and will usually be more forgiving in use than the more expensive specialist lines.

You will need 100 metres of line in each of the strengths that you choose to load your reels with and any line described as 'monofilament' or 'nylon' in strengths approximating those above will be fine.

Line for Hook lengths

It is usual to attach the hook to a line of slightly weaker than that attached to the reel, so that in the event of the line breaking either due to an unexpectedly large fish, or by being caught on an obstruction either in our out of the water, only the short length of line attached to the fish will be lost, resulting in less tackle lost or left attached to a fish.

You will see lines for sale described as for 'hook lengths' but in practice any line that is suitable as reel line will be suitable for hook lengths. In general a hook length of .5 lb (.23 kg) to 1lb (.45 kg) lighter than the reel line will be suitable, so the lines you buy for your reels will determine the additional lines you need to buy for hook lengths.

Fishing Floats

Floats are designed to allow you to see when a fish has taken your bait, but more importantly they are designed to allow you to present a bait to the fish where they are to be found and in as natural a way as possible.

If you look at the floats on offer in a fishing tackle shop you will see that there is an endless variety of floats designed to cover every imaginable fishing situation, but you will also see it written in many fishing books that more floats are made to catch the angler than are made to catch fish!

You need a variety of floats to cover a range of fishing situations, but a few basic patterns and sizes will be sufficient to cover most needs.

Floats for rivers

Generally speaking there are two ways to float fish on a river depending on the distance you need to cast in order to reach the fish.

Top and Bottom Floats

If you do not need to cast a long distance to reach the fish, you will usually attach the float at both the top and bottom by means of plastic or silicon tubing. Three basic patterns will be required to cover these 'top and bottom' fishing situations:

Stick Floats

These are floats constructed in two parts, the top part being of balsa or polystyrene construction and the bottom of either cane or plastic.

Generally speaking, the further you need to cast, the larger the float you will use, but a small range of 'Stick floats' in no more than three or four sizes will be enough to get you started. Avoid the smallest and largest of this type of float, and obtain a few ranging in size from 4 to 6 inches (10 to 15cm) in length.

Balsa Floats

These floats are similar in appearance to Stick Floats, but are more buoyant as they do not incorporate the heavier material in the base that Stick Floats do. These are fished in the same way as Stick floats, but as they take more shot they are suitable for faster water where it is necessary to use a lot of weight to get the bait down to the fish near the bottom.

You can, instead, use a more specialised form of Stick Float referred to as 'Big Sticks' which incorporate a wider buoyant top section to achieve the same purpose. A range of these in lengths from 4 to 6 inches (10 to 15cm) will cover most of your angling needs.

Avon Floats

These are floats that incorporate a large body of balsa or polystyrene or sometimes cork to increase the amount of shot that can be placed on the line. These are mostly used when the river is deep and slow flowing to get the bait down to the fish as quickly as possible.

You will not use these as often as Stick Floats and Balsas, but it is useful to have two or three just in case. A range with shot capacities ranging from 4bb to 6bb will cover most eventualities.

Bottom Only Floats

When you need to cast long distances to reach fish, either in the middle of larger rivers, or close to the far bank, a float attached only at the bottom will cast further and be less likely to tangle.

Straight floats made of plastic, peacock quill or reed and known collectively as Wagglers, are the floats designed for this situation. Wagglers are available in several styles, and types which have a thin piece of can inserted at the top and sometimes incorporates a body near the bottom, is used for fishing lakes and canals as well as slow moving rivers.

For most river fishing you will need a range of straight Wagglers (those with no insert or body) ranging in length from about 5 to 9 inches (12 to 23cm) carrying shot between 2AAA and 6AAA.

In some river fishing situations you can also use Wagglers with inserts or bodies in which case those described in the next section will be suitable.

Floats for lakes and canals

More sensitive floats, that is floats with finer tips, are required for lake and canal fishing than for river fishing, the reason being that when a float is fished in moving water the flow of the current will cause the float to 'go under' or sink when a fish takes the bait. In still water, such as lakes and canals, it is the fish alone that causes the float to 'go under' so a sensitive tip is required to give the least resistance.

A range of straight floats with sensitive tips that are designed to be attached to the line just at the bottom will cover most Stillwater situations. When fishing close to the bank and long casting is not required, small thin floats will be suitable whilst for situations that require long casting to reach the fish, such as on larger lakes or in windy conditions, a thicker float, or one with a buoyant body will be necessary.

These floats are known as 'Insert Wagglers' and 'Bodied Insert Wagglers' and a range covering lengths from 5 to 9 inches (12 to 23cm) carrying shot between 2AAA and 6AAA will be enough to begin with.

Floats for whip fishing

If you have decided to obtain a short pole or whip for close range fishing for small fish as covered earlier, you can use small insert wagglers, but because of the close range at which you will be fishing you can also use specialist pole floats that are designed to be attached to the line at both the top and the bottom.

In appearance these resemble the 'Avon floats' described for river fishing, but in miniature, and have very sensitive tips made or bristle or cane. A few of these will be useful and the ones you want will be about 4 to 5 inches in length (10 to 12 centimetres) with a body near the top of the float about .5 to .75 inches (12mm to 19 mm) in length and about .25 to .5 inches (6mm to 12mm) in width.

Shot

Shot is attached to the line to provide weight to partially sink a float, and can also be used to prevent a leger weight from sliding down the line.

In the past, pieces of lead shot that were manufactured for shotgun cartridges were split to allow them to be pinched on the line, hence the term 'split shot'. Nowadays the use of lead except in the very smallest of sizes is illegal in the UK, so shot is now manufactured specifically for angling purposes using non-toxic alternatives to lead.

You will need shot in a range of sizes, but the sizes most commonly used are SSG, AAA, BBB, Number 1, Number 4, Number 6 and Number 8. You should have no trouble obtaining a single 'dispenser' containing a selection of each of these sizes for about £5.

Leger Weights

Leger weights are attached to the line to allow a bait to be presented on or near the bed of a river or lake. You will need a range of sizes to cover differences in river flow and the distance you need to cast.

There are many types of leger weight, but the most versatile and the only one you need to begin with is a pear shaped weight incorporating a swivel, known as the Arlesey Bomb. Obtain a selection of these in weights from .25 to 1 oz, (7 to 28 grams).

Swimfeeders

Swimfeeders are devices that take the place of leger weights and incorporate a means of getting free offerings of your hookbait or groundbait to the place where you are fishing.

Broadly speaking there are two types, those than are closed at both ends and are mostly used for delivering maggots to the swim and those that are open at both ends and are used to deliver a mix of groundbait (explained later) and maggots, pellets or other baits.

Swimfeeders are not essential to fishing, but if your budget will stretch to it, buy a few of both types in the medium sizes of about 1.5 to 2 inches (3.5 to 5 cm) in length.

Hooks

You will need different sizes of hooks to suit the different baits and species of fish you are intending to catch.

There are many kinds of hooks made in different gauges of wire, both with and without eyes, with and without barbs, and available loose for tying yourself, or already attached to line.

Hook sizes are described using a numerical scale, the higher the number meaning the smaller the hook. This is variable, though, and different manufacturers seem to apply their own rules about how big a hook should be for a given size.

Over time you will find that you need specialised hooks to suit the types of fishing that you do. For now, though, a few sizes and styles will be versatile enough to cover the various fishing situations you encounter, and a range of hooks of sizes 20, 18, 16, 14, 12, 10 and and 8 will be enough to get you started.

There is a lot of controversy about barbed and barbless hooks. One school of thought is that only barbless hooks should be used as they cause less damage to fish. Conversely, some fisheries only allow the use of barbed hooks for the same reason.

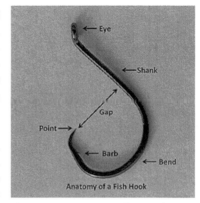

Anatomy of a Fish Hook

We wont go into the debate here, but I would suggest that you obtain both barbed and barbless hooks in the sizes suggested, and you can make up your own mind. As a rule of thumb, when fishing rivers I usually use hooks with a small or 'micro' barb because I think it is less likely that fish will be lost, while for fishing close in on lakes and canals I will usually use barbless hooks as they make unhooking easier.

If for no other reason, barbless hooks are better when you are starting out learning to handle fishing equipment competently as they are easier to remove from nets and clothing than barbed ones. If you start a session using barbless hooks and find that the conditions are causing you to lose fish, you can always change to a barbed hook and see if that improves things.

Initially the pattern of hook you choose is not too important and a range described as general purpose medium wire hooks will be versatile enough to cover most of your fishing.

By all means buy hooks already tied to line if you prefer and can afford it, but for maximum flexibility loose hooks are better as you can then tie them to various strengths of line.

Loose hooks are available both with eyes, and with 'spade' ends. The former can be tied quite easily by hand, whilst the latter are best tied using a tying aid, usually described as a 'Matchman's hook tyer'. Eyed hooks, or those already attached to line may suit you best, as you may feel that you have enough to learn and master already without having to learn to use a hook tying device.

Bait Boxes

For live baits such as maggots and worms a box is necessary and this needs to have small holes to allow for air flow.

Plastic bait boxes are inexpensive and available in a range of sizes. One or two with a capacity of two to three pints will be fine to begin with.

Rod Rests

Rod rests are used to provide a convenient place to put the rod when it is not being held in the hand. When legering or still water float fishing the rod will spend a lot of time in the rests, while for running water fishing they provide a safe and convenient place to put the rod when re-baiting or unhooking a fish.

Rod rests are available either with a male thread to allow them to be screwed into bank sticks, or as a single unit incorporating a V shaped rest, and a metal pole to be pushed into the river bank.

If you are on a very tight budget, the single construction type will suffice, but the screw-in type are generally better and more versatile.

For float fishing it is convenient to have both a front rest and a back rest, especially when still water fishing. For legering you may need both a front rest and a back rest, or just a front rest if you need to point the rod into the air, such as when fishing at range on fast flowing rivers.

Bank Sticks

These are metal poles with a spike at one end and a female threaded section at the other. They are used for both rod rests and keep nets. If you obtain rod rests of the screw-in type, or are intending to use a keep net they are essential, otherwise they are not needed.

General Fishing Items

To complete your kit you can also obtain a number of additional items, some necessary, some optional. Those described here are by no means a comprehensive list, but cover the basics.

The following items fall into the category of 'essential' or 'highly desirable' fishing equipment.

Plummets

These are small weighted devices incorporating either a strip of cork or a hinge to hold the hook while lowering the tackle into the swim to check the depth. These are inexpensive items, and it is useful to have a few as they are easily lost or mislaid when you need them.

Float Caps

As explained in the section on river floats, you will need some plastic or silicon tubing in various thicknesses to attach floats to the line. These are described as 'Float Caps' or 'Float Rubbers' the latter because they were made of rubber before modern materials were available.

You can either buy a packet of pre-cut tubing in mixed sizes, or obtain lengths of plastic or silicon tubing to cut to size when needed.

Float Adapters

These are devices designed to slip over the bottom of 'bottom-only' floats so that if you want to change to a different float during a session you can do so without having to take everything apart.

They are not an essential item by any means as most floats will incorporate a ring for attaching them to the line, but they can save time if a change in conditions means you need to use a heavier float, and they are quite inexpensive.

Some are moulded in one piece from silicon or plastic, and others incorporate a swivel. I've never found much difference in use, so either will do, but it is advisable to get some in different sizes to accommodate different thicknesses of float.

Leger Stops

These are designed to be used to prevent a leger weight or swimfeeder from sliding all of the way down the line to the hook. An alternative method is to pinch a piece of shot on the line. Personally I don't find them necessary, while others swear by them as they believe they are less likely to damage fine line. The choice is yours, but if you're on a tight budget they are not essential.

Swivels

Swivels are devices that are attached to the line in some situations to prevent the line twisting and in some long distance casting situations they can help to avoid tangles. Having a few in your tackle box can be useful, but they are not essential for most general coarse fishing.

They are relatively cheap, and available in a wide range of sizes. For coarse fishing you don't need the very large or very small ones and a few of about 5 to 6 mm will cover those situations where you may need them.

Accessories

The following accessories will be useful as part of your fishing kit:

- A small pair of scissors will be useful for cutting line
- A small penknife has a variety of uses as you will discover.
- Nail clippers are a cheap alternative to specialised line cutters for trimming knots.
- A small pair of pliers can be useful for tackle repairs and loosening corroded screw threads on banksticks and umbrellas.

Specialised Fishing items

There are many specialised items that can be purchased, and whilst not necessarily essential these may be useful.

Beads

Hard beads made of plastic, and soft beads made of rubber or silicon can be useful in constructing rigs for legering.

Silicon Tubing

Silicon tubing is sometimes used in rig construction as well as for attaching floats to line.

Hair rig stops

These are small 'pegs' used to anchor a bait to the line using a 'hair rig'. A hair rig is a term used to describe a tackle arrangement where the bait is not attached to the hook itself, but to a 'hair' of line or other material. At one time hair rigs were only used for carp fishing, but they are now popular for other species such as Barbel.

Bait Bands

These are silicon bands available in a range of sizes that can be used to attach hard baits such pellets, or large baits such as bread flake to the hook.

Baiting Needle

If you intend to use hair rigs a baiting needle with a small hook near the point will be needed to thread baits such as boilies or soft pellets on to the 'hair'.

Tackle for Fish Care

There are some items of fishing tackle that you will need to care for the fish to catch. Some fisheries and clubs insist that you are in possession of some of these items before you are allowed to fish.

Disgorger

This item, which is used to safely remove hooks from fish when they have been swallowed and cannot be removed by hand is an essential item. Disgorgers can be purchased for a few pence each, and you should buy several as they can easily be mislaid. The plastic or nylon variety are best as they will not damage fish. Avoid any that are made of metal and have sharp edges or spikes.

Unhooking Mat

This is used to provide a soft cushioned surface on which to unhook fish. Many fisheries where larger fish are expected insist on an unhooking mat, so check the rules to determine whether you need one.

An unhooking mat is not an essential item of tackle if you are not intending to target larger fish, but if you do catch a large fish that cannot be held safely while unhooking, always make sure you unhook it on a soft cushioned surface to avoid damage if the fish 'jumps' around. If you do not have an unhooking mat, leaving the fish in the landing net and placing it on top of a folded jacket while unhooking will protect the fish from being damaged by a hard bank.

Antiseptic

Many fisheries where large expensive carp are the quarry will insist that you use an antiseptic after unhooking fish. Check the rules to see if this is required where you intend to fish.

Forceps

Metal forceps can be useful for removing hooks that are not easy to remove by hand and are available quite inexpensively. Not essential, but a useful addition to your fishing kit if your budget allows.

Luggage and Seating

When fishing you will need something to sit on and there are a number of specialised chairs and combined seat and tackle carriers available.

What you choose depends on both your budget and the type of fishing you intend to do, but to begin with a stool incorporating a rucksack, or one of the rectangular plastic seat boxes will be fine.

Whatever you choose, remember that you will have to carry it to the bank, so something light and compact that is just big enough to accommodate your fishing tackle and some food or drink will be preferable to an unnecessarily large specialised tackle carrier.

You may also wish to purchase a rod holdall to carry your rods, bank sticks and net pole. You can manage without one to begin with, but basic holdalls are inexpensive and make it less of a chore to carry your tackle over long distances. Before you buy a rod holdall make sure that it is long enough to take your longest rod.

Clothing for Fishing

There is no need to buy specialist angling clothing unless you want to 'look the part'.

It is best to avoid bright colours as you do not want to be any more visible to the fish than you can, but apart from that any outdoor clothing will be suitable.

You will be outside and not moving around a great deal for quite long periods, so make sure that you have sufficient clothing to be warm, and to keep dry if it rains.

In winter, it is best to wear several layers of thin clothing to trap warm air, rather than a single layer of thick clothing. Take care also to ensure that there are no gaps, such as a shirt pulling out of your trousers, as this will create 'cold spots' that are uncomfortable and can result in a lowering of body temperature. A hat is recommended, both for warmth in winter, and so that the peak of a cap, or brim of a hat can shade your eyes from the sun in summer.

Waterproof boots or shoes are also advisable, and in winter it is a good idea to wear an additional pair of thick socks as your feet can become very cold if you are sitting still for long periods of time.

Umbrella

An umbrella will be useful if you intend fishing in all weathers and will be fishing in a single swim for the day, rather than adopting a roving approach, when you will want to be 'travelling light'.

Specialist fishing umbrellas are available with metal spikes allowing them to be driven into the ground for stability.

Prices vary, and some specialist umbrellas are very expensive, but an inexpensive version will do the job until you can afford something better. An umbrella of 45inches (115 cm) or 50 inches (127 metric) can be purchased for £20 or less.

4 GENERAL ADVICE

This section of the guide contains some general advice that you should be aware of before fishing. Some topics will be covered in more detail in later sections, but the purpose of this section is to cover a number of important issues in one place to prepare you for your first fishing trip.

Stealth Tactics

When approaching a swim, and while you are tackling up, keep in mind that fish are cautious creatures. They have many predators and are always alert to danger. If you cause disturbance on the bank, or are visible against the skyline, you may spoil your chances of catching fish.

This is particularly important when approaching swims on small rivers, or where the water is very clear.

Tackle up away from the bank side and set up your tackle with the minimum possible disturbance. Just because you cannot see the fish, doesn't mean they cannot see you, and if you can see the fish, they can almost certainly see you.

Make use of bank side cover to hide your presence from the fish. That doesn't just mean cover in front of you – positioning yourself in front of a bank side feature such as a high bank, bush or tree behind you will disguise you, especially if you wear drab clothing that helps you to blend in.

Care of Tackle

Good fishing tackle will last many seasons if it is well cared for.

Rods and reels should be thoroughly dried after a fishing session to prevent corrosion and mould. Rods should not be stored for any length of time in wet rod bags.

Some reels benefit from being oiled occasionally, and you should dismantle them to clean out any dirt or grit that has accumulated at least once a season.

Check rod rings frequently for wear, and replace any where the ring has broken or worn. Check the whippings too, and re-whip rings if they have become loose. Many good fish have been lost because these simple precautions have not been observed.

Floats are designed to be waterproof, but should be checked for cracks and splits in the varnish that could allow water to seep in. Varnish and paints for repairs are inexpensive and easily obtained from hardware stores and craft shops.

Keep hooks and other tackle items dry. It is surprising how much water can get into tackle boxes on a rainy day, so check when you get home, and if necessary allow everything to dry thoroughly before storing it away again.

Umbrellas should be dried thoroughly after use too, there is nothing worse than an umbrella that cannot be properly assembled due to corrosion as you will only find out there is a problem when you need protection from the next downpour on the bank!

Loading Line on to a reel

Line should be loaded on to the reel so that it almost reaches the edge of the spool. A reel that is not loaded with enough line will be difficult to cast with, and reasonable distances will be hard to achieve.

Some reels have narrow spools that only need 100 metres of line to fill them, but others have deep spools and these need to be loaded with backing before attaching the fishing line. You can buy specialist backing, but any old line will do to fill out a spool if you have some.

An alternative to using backing or old line is to wrap self-adhesive tape around the spool, but if you do this, make sure that you apply the tape uniformly so the line will wind evenly on the spool.

Assembling a Rod

To anyone who has fished for any length of time, this piece of advice will seem so obvious that it hardly needs saying, but in my experience, unless told, many new Anglers just don't think about it.

Many rods are made in three sections and have to be assembled before fishing. This involves pushing the different sections together and lining up the rod rings.

It is much easier to assemble the two thinnest sections first, and then connect these to the thickest or butt section, than assembling the two thickest sections first, as it avoids you having to 'climb up the rod' to attach the end section!

Threading line through the rod rings

When threading line through the rod rings, make sure the bale arm of the reel is open, and the anti-reverse is in the off position.

With long rods you will not be able to reach the reel once you have threaded line through half of the rings and the bale arm may close if a bank side obstruction causes it to flip over or turns the reel handle.

If this happens you should be able to finish threading the rings by gently pulling on the line to cause the reel handle to turn and give line.

Although this may seem unlikely to happen, you will be surprised how often it does!

Casting Techniques

There are two main casting techniques that you will need to master, the overhead cast, and the underarm cast.

There are no hard and fast rules about which cast you should use for a given situation and you will quickly develop your own style, but in general terms you would use the overhead cast when you need to cast a long distance, and the underarm cast when long distance casting is not required, and you are fishing with tackle that could easily tangle if you used an overhead cast, such as a stick float rig.

Overhead Cast

This is probably the easier of the two to learn as timing is less important than with the underhand cast. A poorly timed overhead cast will, unless it is really badly mis-timed, just result in less distance, and a bigger splash when the tackle hits the water.

To begin the cast, let out enough line so that you can comfortably swing the tackle by moving the rod backwards and forwards. Open the bail arm of the spool so that the line can run off, and prevent this by trapping the line against the spool with your finger.

Next, lift the rod to a vertical position so that it is pointing straight up. The next part requires practice to get the timing just right so don't worry if your initial attempts don't go too well.

Imagine that you are standing next to a large clock face, and the rod is currently pointing to 12 o'clock.

In one fluid movement, swing the tackle behind you by moving the rod sharply back so that it is pointing at between 10 and 11 o'clock, and then immediately move the rod sharply forwards so that it is pointing at between 1 and 2 o'clock. Stop the rod, and release the line by lifting your finger off the spool.

If you get the timing right, the tackle should be propelled away from you towards the place where you want to fish, and if the spool is loaded correctly, line should come off the spool freely.

When the tackle is a few inches above the water, drop the rod tip to between 3 and 4 o'clock, and the tackle should land gently on the surface without causing too much disturbance.

The most difficult part of the cast is timing the release of the line correctly. If you release too early, the line will fly up in the air without the necessary power, and will land in a heap. Release too late, and the tackle will not achieve the required distance and will be driven with excessive force into the water.

Underhand Cast

This cast will not achieve the same distance as the overhead cast, but it does give you more control over the tackle in flight, and is less likely to result in the tackle becoming tangled.

To begin the cast, assuming you are right handed, hold the rod in your right hand, open the bail arm of the reel, and let out enough line from the rod tip so that with your left hand you can comfortably hold the line just above the hook.

Hold the rod across your body while keeping the line under tension with your left hand, and then flick the rod towards the water so that it is pointing directly away from you, at the same time releasing the line held in your left hand. You should find that the tackle is propelled towards the place you want to fish, and if you get enough power into the cast, and get your timing right, line should flow off the spool.

Timing of this cast is quite difficult to master, but with practice you will find that it becomes second nature. As your skills progress you will find that you can achieve this cast holding the rod at different angles to avoid bank side vegetation and other obstacles.

Striking or Setting the Hook

Striking is the term used to describe the action of setting the hook in the fish when you get a bite.

It is not usually necessary to do more than move the rod swiftly back a few inches with a flick, but when fishing at range, or if there is a lot of slack line between you and your tackle, you may need to strike with a sweeping action to pick up the slack line and make contact with the fish.

Speed of the strike is much more important than power as all you are trying to do is pull the hook firmly into the mouth of the fish before it has time to eject the bait.

As a general rule, keep in mind that the closer in you are fishing, the less powerfully you need to strike.

An unnecessarily powerful strike when fishing at close range will result in your tackle being pulled out of the water, sometimes with a small fish attached! There is no surer way that I know of to get your tackle in a tangle!

Playing Fish

Small fish can be wound in quite easily and then swung to hand, but large fish are capable of long sustained fights during which you may have to give line.

When you hook a large fish, do not try to bully it out of the water as quickly as possible, your aim is to tire the fish so that when all of the fight has gone out of it, you can draw it safely over the landing net.

Large fish will try to swim away from you as fast as they can when they are hooked, or soon after as they feel resistance. You will usually need to give line to prevent a break or the hook pulling free and this can be done in two ways.

Most reels are equipped with a slipping clutch. This allows the spool to rotate to give line when the pull is approaching that which would break the line. An alternative is to allow the fish to take line under pressure by winding the reel backwards. Personally I prefer to backwind, using judgement to determine when giving line is necessary. If you do choose to use the slipping clutch, make sure it is set to just below the breaking strain of the line. Too slack and you will struggle to recover line, too tight and you risk a break.

Playing a fish is a little like a tug of war match. You give a little, you gain a little until eventually the fish is tired. To gain the maximum advantage from your tackle it is essential that you use the rod to cushion the lunges of the fish, so most of the time you should hold it high. This applies maximum pressure on the fish, and also prevents it from coming too high in the water before it is ready for the net.

The exception to this is when you need to stop a fish from reaching an obstruction such as a weed bed or some tree roots. If you lock down the reel and try to stop the fish by holding the rod high you may pull out the hook or break the line. When you need to stop a fish in this way, drop the rod tip so you are applying 'side strain'. Usually this will force the fish up nearer the surface and is often enough to make it change direction away from the snag.

Learning to play a fish well is something that only experience can teach you, but with perseverance you will develop an instinct for when a fish is ready to be brought to the net.

Landing Fish

When a fish is tired you will notice that its lunges and runs become weaker and shorter. This can be the most dangerous part of the fight, as the fish will be closer and nearer the surface and you have only a short amount of line between you and the fish.

Very often, a fish that has been brought to the surface will make a desperate lunge for freedom as soon as it sees you or the net, so be prepared to give more line and continue the fight when this happens.

Eventually the fish will be beaten and will turn sideways on the surface. Now is the time to slip the net under the fish and draw it back from the water.

Do not drag the fish for a long distance to the net, try to get the net as close to the fish and draw it over the lip of the net in a steady controlled movement. When fishing fast rivers you may need to position the net a little downstream of the fish, and allow the current to take the fish over the net. Never try to pull a beaten fish against the current as that is a sure way of pulling out the hook.

Once the fish is in the net, draw the net back in the water to ensure the fish is safely in the folds. You should then disengage the bale arm on the reel and place the rod in its rest so you have both hands free to lift the net.

Do not lift the net out of the water while you are still holding the end of the pole as it will bend, and could break. Instead, slide the pole backwards until you can safely lift it out of the water by gripping the pole with both hands near the net.

Unhooking Fish

Small fish can be safely unhooked in the hand after being swung in, larger fish should be unhooked while lying on the bank supported on a soft surface such as an unhooking mat.

Be careful when unhooking fish not to grip them too tightly, and only handle them with damp hands to prevent removal of slime.

Most of the time a fish will be hooked in the lip, and the hook can be easily removed by hand. Grip the shank of the hook between finger and thumb and gently pull it out. Barbless hooks will come out easily, but barbed hooks may need to be removed by very gently shaking the hook at the same time as pulling to release the grip of the barb.

If the fish is hooked deeper in the mouth and you cannot reach it with your fingers, you may need to use forceps to grimly grip the hook to remove it using the same technique as above.

Using a Disgorger

When a fish has swallowed the hook and you cannot see it to grip it with forceps you will need to use a disgorger. You should make sure that you have several of these in your fishing kit and jacket so you can quickly lay your hands on one when needed. Some anglers have a disgorger on a piece of string round their neck, or on a cord attached to their jacket so it is close to hand.

A disgorger is simple to use, but takes a little practice. Keep the line under gentle tension by wrapping it around a finger of the hand that is holding the disgorger. Then, slide the disgorger on to the line using the slot in the side, and gently push the disgorger down the line until you feel the resistance of the hook.

A further gentle push should dislodge the hook, and you should then turn the disgorger by about 25 degrees and pull it back out of the fish. It should come out with no resistance, so if it will not come out easily, the hook has not been dislodged and you need to repeat the process.

Returning Fish to the Water

It is important that you do not throw fish back into the water as they are fragile creatures and could be damaged. Instead, gently slip the fish into the water nose first and it should swim away strongly.

On high banks you may not be able to reach the water, so return the fish by lowering it to the surface in your landing net and gently turning it out.

Some fish, notably Barbel, need time to recover before they can swim away and you may need to support them with their noses pointed into the current until you feel them swim away from you.

If you use a keep net, release the fish at the end of the session by gently lifting the end of the net furthest from the mouth so the fish swim out. Do not allow fish to flap around in the bottom of a net out of water as the larger fish will damage themselves, and other smaller fish below them.

If you want to weigh your fish after a session you will need to remove them from the net while it is out of water. Some keep nets have a ring that allows the bottom of the net to be lifted out of the mouth so fish can be removed safely. If your keep net does not have this feature, move the fish as near to the mouth of the net as possible using the method in the previous paragraph before gently tipping them into the weighing net. The head of a landing net can be used to weigh fish if you do not have a specialist weighing net or basket.

5 FISHING METHODS

The purpose of this section of the guide is to briefly explain the different methods that you can use to catch fish in a variety of locations. More detail on each type of fishing can be found in the following section describing different fishing rigs.

Float Fishing

Float fishing is a technique where the baited hook is suspended above the bed of the lake, river or canal using a float made of buoyant material. Shot is used to cause the float to 'sit' in the water with only the tip visible above the surface.

A bite is detected by watching for the float to be partially or completely submerged by a biting fish.

Float Fishing on Lakes and Canals

When float fishing on lakes and canals the float is attached to the line at the bottom using shot. This is known as 'bottom only'.

More sensitive floats are required than for river fishing, as the fish alone is responsible for pulling the float down in the water as there is no current, so floats with thin tips, sometimes inserted into a thicker body are used.

The remaining shot required to sink the float so only the tip is showing are then placed on the line between the float and the hook. If you want the bait to sink slowly so that fish feeding up in the water can intercept it, the shot is spaced out, but if you want to get the bait down to the bottom quickly, perhaps because a lot of small fish near the surface are taking the bait before it can reach larger fish below, the shot will be bunched closer to the hook.

After casting the float to the desired fishing spot, the line needs to be sunk so that the float is not dragged around by surface drift or wind. To do this, immediately after casting drop the tip of the rod in the water, and lift it sharply up. This should cause the line between the rod and the float to be pulled beneath the surface. An alternative, if this proves difficult, is to cast beyond the place where you want to fish, and then dip the rod tip in the water, and wind a couple of sharp turns of the reel.

Once the float is in position and the line submerged, the rod should be placed in two rests such that the handle of the rod is conveniently to hand for striking, and the tip is in or near the water to prevent any loose line from being affected by wind.

Watch the float carefully for bites. It may dip quickly under the water, but more often you will see the float dip slightly, move to one side, or even come up in the water. All are signals to strike, which should be done by sharply lifting the rod tip up to set the hook.

When fishing in still-water, the size of float you decide to fish with is determined by the distance you plan to fish at, whether you are casting into a head wind or cross wind and the depth of water.

You should be able to cast comfortably to the place you wish to fish, so if you are finding this difficult or if the wind increases, switch to a larger float or one with a body at the base so you can put more shot on the line. When fishing deep water a larger float may be needed to allow more shot to be placed on the line to get the bait down to the bottom more quickly.

You should always find out the depth using a plummet, and it is usually best to start by fishing on or near the bottom, but if fish are in the upper levels of water you will often get bites 'on the drop' while the baited hook is falling through the water. If the fish are small, you can move the bulk shot nearer the hook to get a faster fall through the water, or even reduce the size of the locking shot to allow more bulk shot to be placed on the line.

If, on the other hand, it is the fish you wish to catch that are feeding up in the water, moving the shot higher up the line and shortening the line between the float and the hook will ensure that your baited hook stays longer in the feeding zone.

Unlike river float fishing it is the fish alone that pulls the float under the surface when you get a bite, so you should use the thinnest tip that conditions allow. The thicker the tip, the more pull a fish needs to exert to pull it under. A thinner tip will be pulled further beneath the surface making bites easier to spot, whereas a thick tip may hardly move, and worse may cause resistance that the fish can feel resulting in it ejecting the bait before you have time to strike.

If you are having trouble hitting bites, it pays to adjust the position of the small 'dropper' shot either nearer to the hook or further away until you find the distance that results in the most bites being hit.

While the tackle is in the water, you will keep the bail arm of the reel closed to prevent line being blow off by wind. Whether you also engage the reel's anti-reverse mechanism is a matter of personal choice. If you do, there is no risk of the strike being cushioned by line being pulled off the reel, but you will need to disengage the anti-reverse to play large fish. If you leave the anti-reverse in the off position you will not have to do this, but you will need to trap the spool of the reel with your finger when striking to prevent line being given when you strike.

Float Fishing on Rivers

When float fishing on rivers you will usually attach the float to the line using silicon or plastic tubing placed at both ends of the float. This is known as 'top and bottom' or 'double rubber'.

Shot is then attached to the line between the float and the hook, either spaced out or in bunches so that only the tip of the float is visible above the water.

The tackle is then swung out into the stream and allowed to float down the river with the current.

You need to continually pay put line with this method, so the bale arm of the reel is left open and the line is controlled by pressure applied with your finger at the edge of the spool.

To keep a tight line to the float you may need to 'mend the line' by trapping the line with your finger and lifting the rod until the line between the rod tip and float is straight. On rivers where the flow is slow and there are many surface currents you may need to do this several times on each passage of the float down the swim.

This technique is referred to as 'trotting', and when the float needs to travel a long way down the swim to reach the fish, it is known as 'long trotting'.

When you get a bite, trap the line against the spool with your finger and strike with a sweeping movement away from the float. The further away the float is, the more powerful the strike, but often it is only necessary to stop the float as the current will set the hook.

Another river float fishing method involves the use of a Waggler float that is only attached to the line at the bottom. This allows the float to be cast further without risk of tangles on wide rivers, or when you want to fish near the far bank.

With this method it is not possible to keep a tight line to the float as this would cause it to be pulled towards you and the bait would not appear to be behaving naturally to the fish.

Instead of mending the line, you allow a bow to form between the rod tip and float, and you then 'feed the bow' by paying out enough line to allow the float to move unhindered down the swim.

A more powerful strike is required with this method as you have to recover all of the line in the bow before making contact with the fish. This is achieved by a high sweeping movement of the rod over your shoulder.

With both methods, as soon as a fish is hooked you have to decide whether you need to allow it to take line before you close the bail arm of the reel in preparation for winding in or playing the fish. If it is a small fish you can immediately close the bail arm and commence winding. If you feel resistance from a large fish, allow it to take line with the bail arm open, and close it only when you feel the fish stop its initial run.

When fishing with running line tackle on rivers, make sure that the anti-reverse on the reel is set to the off position if you intend to give line by winding backwards rather than using the slipping clutch.

Legering

Legering is a technique where the baited hook is fished on or near the bed of the river, lake or canal by means of a weight that is attached to the line.

A bite is detected by watching the tip of the rod for a pull caused by a biting fish. Bites may also be detected by holding the line between finger and thumb.

Legering on Lakes and Canals

When legering on still waters, it is usual to fish with a swimfeeder so that you can introduce ground bait and loose feed into the swim near your bait.

Still water legering is a popular technique for catching Bream which are bottom feeders, but this technique will catch many species of fish, and is sometimes necessary when you need to cast further than is possible with float tackle.

As you will be introducing feed into the swim on every cast, it is important that your tackle always lands in roughly the same area to avoid spreading feed widely over the bottom which would result in the fish not being concentrated where you are fishing.

You will normally use the overhead cast to achieve maximum distance, and the first part of ensuring that your tackle always lands in roughly the same place is to choose a marker on the opposite bank, and cast towards that each time.

When you are first starting out, that is probably all you should concentrate on, relying on judgment to cast approximately the same distance each time, but as you progress, you can use rubber bands or line clips to prevent line from being taken from the spool once you have cast the required distance.

For still water fishing you should use the finest tip that came with your leger rod, and you need to position the rod in two rod rests more or less parallel to the bank, so that an angle of about 90 degrees is formed between the tip of the rod and your tackle. This will give the maximum indication on the tip when you get bites.

After casting out, wait a few seconds after the tackle hits the water to allow the leger or swimfeeder to reach the bottom, and then close the bail arm on the reel. Next position the rod in the rests and take up the slack line so that the line between the rod tip and your tackle is tight.

You are now ready to watch the tip for indications of a bite which make come in the form of a pull or tap, or a slackening of the line caused by a fish picking up the bait and swimming towards you.

When you get a bite, lift the rod out of the rests and strike with a sharp movement of the rod away from the tackle.

If bites are coming slowly you may need to re-cast regularly to get a decent amount of ground bait and loose feed into the swim.

Legering on Rivers

When legering on slow rivers you can use a similar technique to that described for still water legering. On fast rivers, however, a differentmethod is required.

When the pull of the current is strong, you need to take this into account when deciding the weight of leger or swimfeeder to use. You need to use

just enough weight to prevent the tackle being dislodged and carried down the swim.

You will need to use a heavier quivertip than for still water legering as the pull of a strong current will bend a light tip round making bite detection difficult, and you may also need to position the rod in one rest, pointing up at an angle of about 45 degrees to the water to relieve the water pressure on the line which could dislodge your tackle.

When you are ready cast out the tackle as described for still water legering, and allow time for the tackle to reach the bottom before closing the bailarm and positioning the rod in the rest.

You should then take up any slack line, but in some conditions it may be necessary to leave a bow in the line between the tip and the leger or swimfeeder due to the pull of the current.

As with still water legering, bites may come in the form of a pull or slackening of the line, which is your indication to strike. You will find, though, that fish often hook themselves when you are fishing in strong currents, and all that is necessary is for you to lift the rod and begin playing the fish.

Pike Fishing

Whilst Pike can be caught using float fishing and legering methods, different rigs to those used for other coarse fish are called for.

Fishing with Live and Dead Baits

Both live and dead baits will catch Pike, but check the rules before fishing as many clubs and associations do not allow livebaiting on their waters.

Live baits, such as small Roach can be fished 'free roaming' using heavy float gear, or on a paternoster float leger rig, where the live bait is attached to a swivel part way between the float and the leger weight. See the section on rigs for further explanation. The same float and float leger rigs can also be used with dead baits, but another successful method is to fish dead baits using a standard bottom fishing leger rig. Again, an example of this type of tackle set up is shown in the section on rigs.

Fishing with Artificial Baits

Many Pike are caught using artificial baits, known as Lures, using a technique generally called Spinning. There is a wide variety of artificial Lures available, and these are fished by drawing them through the water to imitate a fish.

To describe in detail how to fish the various types of lures that are available in a wide variety of waters would require a book to itself, but in principle, you attach the lure to your main line using a wire trace (Pike have sharp teeth that could easily cut through line), cast it out to the desired starting point, and then wind it back in while changing the rate of retrieve to simulate the swimming action of a live fish. See Pike in the section on British Coarse Fish for more information on Lure fishing.

6 COMMON FISHING TECHNIQUES AND RIGS

In this chapter various rigs for fishing rivers and stillwaters are explained using diagrams. Although these rigs will give you a good starting point, unless bites are coming thick and fast, you should always be prepared to experiment. If you are float fishing, moving the shots on the line could bring more bites, and if legering try moving the leger stop to increase or decrease the distance from the weight to the hook.

Succesful anglers don't sit and wait for the bites to come, they constantly experiment to find out what the fish want on a particular day.

River stick float rig

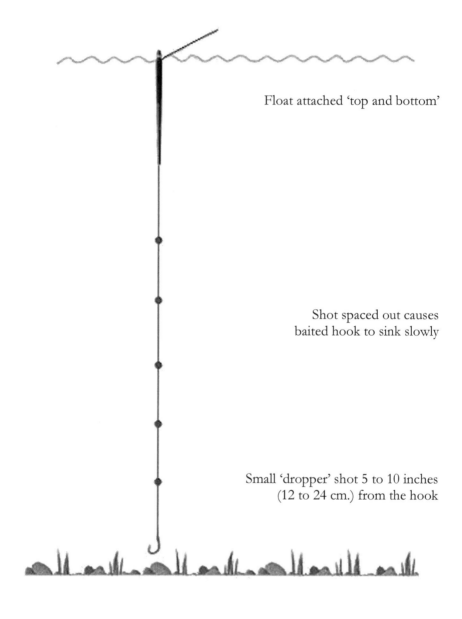

Float attached 'top and bottom'

Shot spaced out causes
baited hook to sink slowly

Small 'dropper' shot 5 to 10 inches
(12 to 24 cm.) from the hook

River balsa or big stick rig

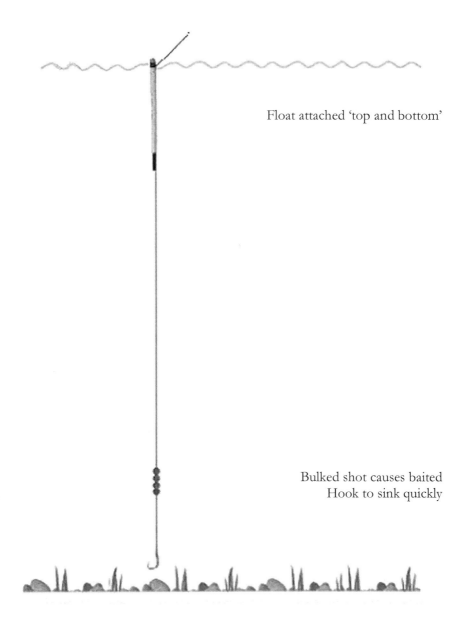

Float attached 'top and bottom'

Bulked shot causes baited
Hook to sink quickly

River avon rig

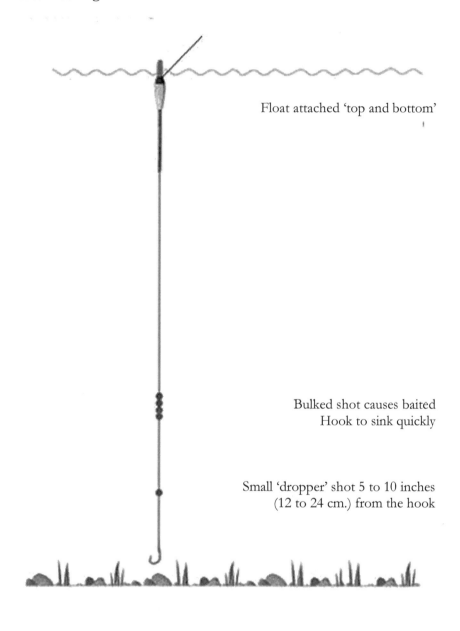

Float attached 'top and bottom'

Bulked shot causes baited
Hook to sink quickly

Small 'dropper' shot 5 to 10 inches
(12 to 24 cm.) from the hook

River waggler rig

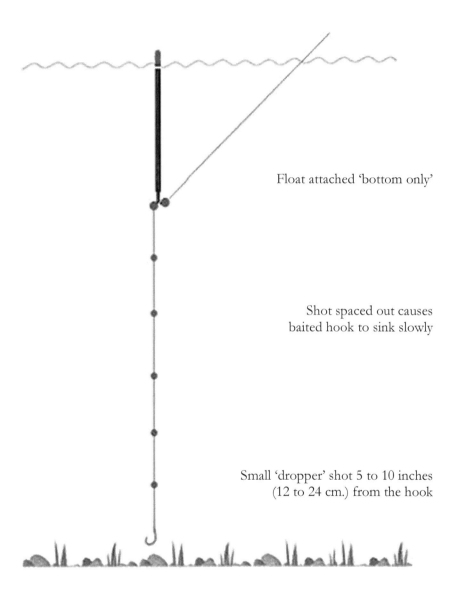

Float attached 'bottom only'

Shot spaced out causes
baited hook to sink slowly

Small 'dropper' shot 5 to 10 inches
(12 to 24 cm.) from the hook

Stillwater insert waggler rig

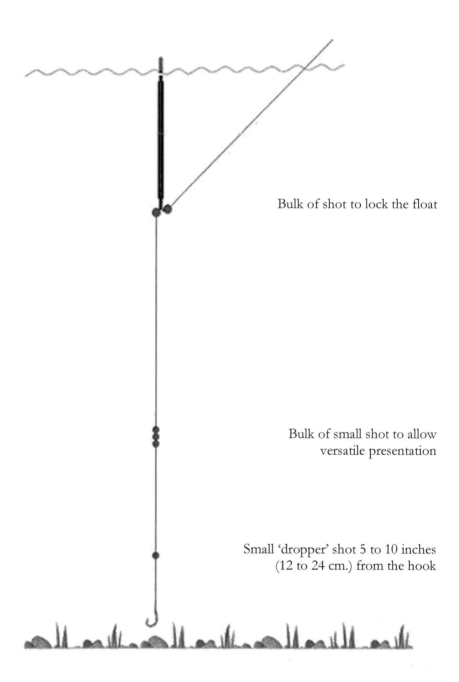

Bulk of shot to lock the float

Bulk of small shot to allow
versatile presentation

Small 'dropper' shot 5 to 10 inches
(12 to 24 cm.) from the hook

Stillwater bodied waggler rig

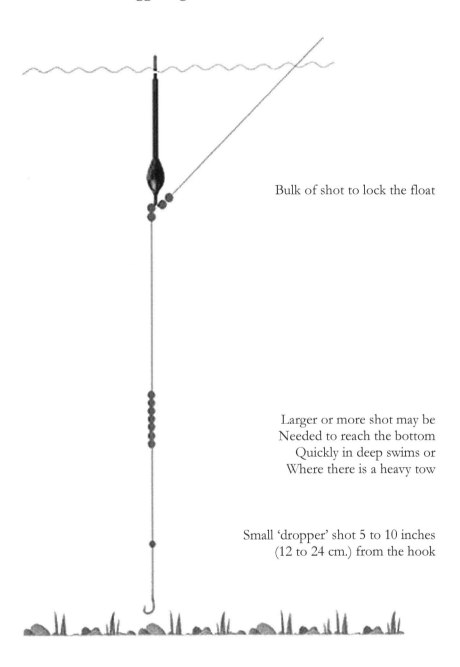

Bulk of shot to lock the float

Larger or more shot may be
Needed to reach the bottom
Quickly in deep swims or
Where there is a heavy tow

Small 'dropper' shot 5 to 10 inches
(12 to 24 cm.) from the hook

Whip rig for fishing 'on the drop'

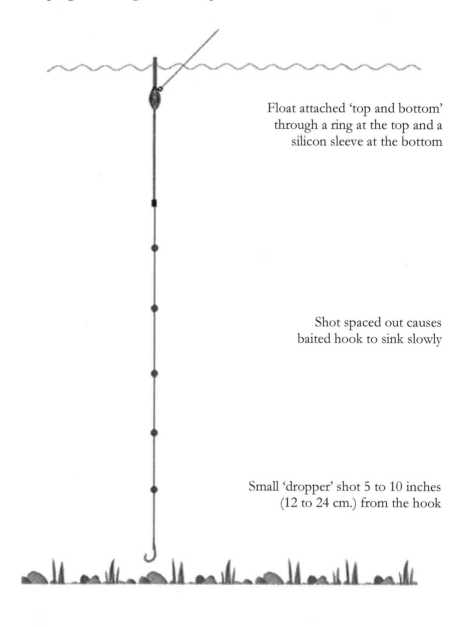

Float attached 'top and bottom' through a ring at the top and a silicon sleeve at the bottom

Shot spaced out causes baited hook to sink slowly

Small 'dropper' shot 5 to 10 inches (12 to 24 cm.) from the hook

Whip Rig for fishing on or near the bottom

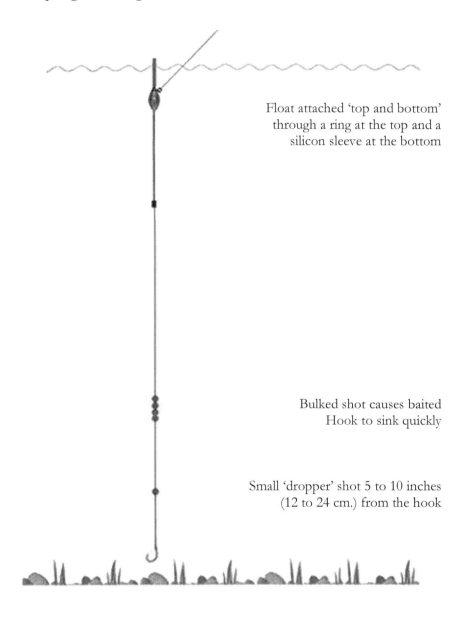

Float attached 'top and bottom'
through a ring at the top and a
silicon sleeve at the bottom

Bulked shot causes baited
Hook to sink quickly

Small 'dropper' shot 5 to 10 inches
(12 to 24 cm.) from the hook

Simple running leger rig

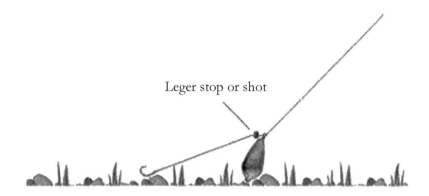

Leger stop or shot

Loop method swimfeeder rig

Swimfeeder runs freely on
loop to minimise resistance

7 BAITS, GROUND BAITS AND FLAVOURINGS

A wide variety of items can be used to catch fish and attract them into your swim. Some of these are specialist items that you can buy at fishing tackle shops, but there are also many household food items that can be used either as they are, or to make good fishing baits.

Hook Baits

This section lists a variety of baits that can be used on the hook to catch a wide range of fish species. Most of these are also used a loose feed that is fed into the swim to attract fish, and encourage them to feed on the bait on your hook.

Maggots

Maggots are the easiest bait to use, and will catch just about any fish that swims.

Three types of maggots are usually available in fishing tackle shops, described as Maggots, Pinkies and Squatts.

The largest kind, just called Maggots, are good for most fishing situations, both for use on the hook and to throw in as 'loose feed' to attract fish into your swim and keep them there.

A smaller variety of maggot called Pinkies are good for canals and lakes and can be used as both hook and loose feed, or just as loose feed in conjunction with larger Maggots on the hook.

Squatts are the smallest maggots available commercially and are very popular as a loose feed with Bream Anglers who introduce them into the swim with groundbait. They can also be a useful hook bait when fish are small or reluctant to take a larger Maggot.

All types of Maggot need to be kept cool and will keep best if stored in a refrigerator. If you do keep them in a refrigerator do not use a lid as this will keep them cooler and prevent them from escaping.

Maggots can also be stored in plastic containers such as the special bait boxes that can be obtained from fishing tackle shops.eep them in a cool place such as a garage or shed.

Casters

Casters are the chrysalis form of the maggot and can be purchased from tackle shops or 'turned' from maggots left over from a fishing trip.

Casters will not keep for long periods unless refrigerated as they will float which makes them useless for most types of fishing. They also need to be kept cool while fishing, and Anglers usually keep them in a bait box filled with enough water to just cover them.

Casters will catch most coarse fish, and will sometimes allow you to avoid small fish which may take them less readily than the larger specimens.

Worms

All types of worm will catch fish, and these can be collected yourself or purchased from fishing tackle shops.

Large lob worms can be collected from damp grass at night, and these, together with commercially available Dendrobaenas make good baits for large fish.

Redworms and Brandlings can be found in compost heaps and are a very versatile bait for most species.

Bread Flake

A piece of flake pinched from the middle of a fresh loaf is an excellent bait for Chub and Roach as well as other species.

Bread Crust

A piece of bread crust fished to float on the surface of a river is a popular bait for Chub, and also for Carp on still waters.

Bread Paste

A paste made from bread will catch many species of fish and is a particularly good bait on some waters for Roach and Chub.

To make bread paste, take a few slices from a fresh loaf and either tear it into small pieces, or chop it up in a liquidiser. To this, add sufficient water to make a soft dough, and knead it until it is smooth.

It is not necessary to colour or flavour bread paste, but some Anglers add sugar or honey to give the paste a sweet flavour. It can also be coloured using ordinary food colouring, yellow and red being popular colours.

Cheese and Cheese Paste

Hard cheese, such as cheddar can be kneaded until soft and moulded around a hook. This is a favourite bait with Chub Anglers but will take other species too.

A paste made of bread and cheese is also a good bait.

Luncheon Meat

Luncheon meat is a good bait for Carp, Barbel and Chub. It can be used in cubes or strips or rough chunks. The cheapest brands are best s these are firmer and will stay on the hook better.

Boilies

A wide range of commercial boilies are available and your fishing tackle shop will be able to advise you of local preferences. The larger sizes are used to catch large carp, while the smaller sizes will catch a variety of coarse fish.

Pellets

A wide range of pellets in various sizes, colours and flavours are available from fishing tackle shops, designed to catch most species of coarse fish.

Sweetcorn

Sweetcorn, either from a tin or frozen is a good bait for many coarse fish species. You can also obtain coloured or flavoured sweetcorn from fishing tackle shops.

It is sometimes necessary to use dyed sweetcorn on waters where it has been heavily used and the fish are wary of it. You can with buy it coloured, or soak some sweetcorn in food colouring to dye it yourself. Red is a popular colour where fish have become of the natural bait.

Seed and Nut Baits

Hempseed is widely available either in cooked or uncooked form, and is an excellent bait for many species. It is most often used as loose feed to attract fish into a swim and hold them there while fished in conjunction with other hook baits, but a single grain of hemp seed on the hook can be an excellent bait for roach.

There are also a number of other seed and nut baits available from fishing tackle shops where you will be able to get advice on the best baits to use on your local waters.

Dog Biscuits

Dog biscuits are a popular bait with Carp Anglers who use them to catch surface feeding Carp.

Live Baits

Small coarse fish such as Roach, Rudd, Bream, Gudgeon and Minnows are suitable for use when fishing for Pike, Perch or Zander where live baiting is permitted.

Dead Baits

Coarse and sea fish can be used as dead baits for Pike and Zander. Small fish such as Sprats can be used whole, while larger fish such as Mackerel are usually cut into strips or chunks.

Artificial Baits

There are many kinds of artificial baits designed to imitate small fish for catching predatory fish such as Pike and Zander. These are designed for a variety of fishing techniques and can float, sink or be made to dive in the water. More traditional patterns are known as Spinners, Spoons and Plugs and more recently a range of soft plastic baits known as Jellies which very accurately imitate fish have become available.

A wide range of artificial baits are also available to imitate natural baits such as Maggots, Sweetcorn, Bread and Dog Biscuits. These can be very effective when fished in conjunction with the real thing if feeding freely and are not being very selective, or if small fish are destroying a large bait such as bread or Dog Biscuits before the larger fish can reach it.

Ground Baits

Ground bait is a term given to a soft paste or dough that you introduce into a swim to encourage fish to forage for food. Ground bait is made by mixing very fine particles of cereal and other materials with water to produce a dough that will break up in the water.

Sometimes ground bait is used to form a cloud of particles in the water, and sometimes it is designed to form an artificial bed over which fish will feed.

When fishing at range samples of your hook bait can be added to groundbait to allow it to be thrown into the swim or introduced in an open ended swimfeeder.

Commercial Ground Baits

A wide range of commercial groundbaits are available from fishing tackle shops. Different types of groundbait will behave differently when introduced to the swim and you should study the instructions on the packet or seek advice to determine which will be suitable for the waters you intend to fish.

Ground Bait Additives

A wide range of powdered and liquid groundbait additives are available to colour and flavour groundbait. You can also mix different types of groundbait to make your own preferred mix.
Making your own Ground Baits
You can make your own groundbait using bread.

A good groundbait can be made by liquidising a few slices of bread. As bread in this form is quite moist it is not necessary to mix it with water as it can easily be formed into balls to throw into the swim.

Liquidised bread is a good bait where Roach or Chub are the intended quarry, but when Roach fishing take care not to introduce too much to the swim as it can be very filling.

You can also make a very effective groundbait by drying slices of old, but not stale, white or brown bread in the oven and using a liquidiser to break it into very fine particles.

This can then be mixed with water and introduced in balls into the swim. Use less water if you want the groundbait to break up quickly and form a cloud, more water if you want the groundbait to break up on the bottom.

Flavourings

A wide variety of artificial flavourings are available in fishing tackle shops to flavour both ground bait and hook baits.

You can also flavour baits with a variety of household food products, and some of the popular ones are listed below.

Flavourings for Bread Paste

- Honey
- Sugar
- Cheese paste
- Cheese Powder
- Crushed trout pellet

Flavourings for Maggots

- Curry powder, especially when winter fishing for Roach or Chub
- Turmeric which also dyes them a deep yellow/gold colour
- Fenugreek, less popular now but at one time a favourite

8 KNOTS FOR FISHING

There are many knots that are suitable for fishing, but you need only learn a few to begin with to be equipped for any fishing situation.

Joining two lengths of line

There are two common methods for joining two lengths of line, e.g. to attach a short length of lighter hook length line to the main line.

Loop Method

The simplest method of joining two lengths of line is to use two loops tied using a Surgeon's loop knot.

To tie a Surgeons loop knot, first double the line back on itself to form a loop. Next form a loop using the doubled line and pass the end through this larger loop two or three times.

Finally, moisten the line and pull tight.

The loop on the hook length is threaded through the loop on the main line and the hook is threaded back through the hook length loop and pulled tight.

Double Fisherman's Knot

An alternative method that you can use when you do not want to use loops is the double fisherman's knot.

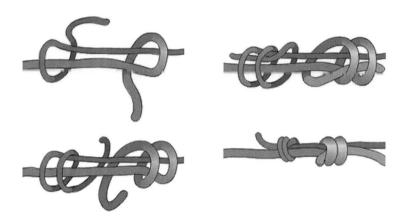

It is a good idea to moisten the knot before pulling tight as this will lubricate the line and prevent it from being weakened by heat damage caused by friction.

Attaching hooks to line

Hooks that are not purchased already tied to line can be attached using the knot described below. Small spade end hooks are more easily tied using a Hook Tyer, an inexpensive accessory available from fishing tackle shops.

Bumper Knot

This knot can be used to tie either eyed or spade end hooks. If tying an eyed hook, first pass the line through the eye of the hook.

9 FISHING CHECKLIST

The following checklist will help to ensure that you don't arrive on the bank of your favourite river or lake without everything you need.

Antiseptic (if Carp fishing)
Bait and ground bait
Bait Bands
Baiting Needle
Bank Sticks (for rod rests and keep nets)
Beads
Disgorgers
Float Adapters
Float Caps (silicon tubing for attaching floats)
Floats
Food and drink
Forceps
Ground Bait
Hair Rig Stops
Hooks
Keep Net
Landing Net

Leger Stops
Leger Weights
Line for hook lengths
Line clippers
Penknife
Pliers
Plummets
Reel
Rod
Rod rests
Scissors
Seat (if not using a seat box)
Swimfeeders
Swivels
Towel
Umbrella
Unhooking Mat
Waterproof Clothing

10 SPECIES OF COARSE FISH

This section describes the various species of coarse fish that you will encounter when fishing and some baits and tactics that can be used to catch them.

Barbel

Latin name Barbus barbus

The barbel is a long bodied fish with a prominent snout flanked on each side by two barbels.

The Barbel is generally a shoal fish, but some rivers contain small groups of very large specimens.

Whilst Barbel have been present in British waters for a considerable time, their colonisation of some rivers systems, notably the River Severn system is relatively recent following stocking.

In the 1970's Barbel became the dominant species in some parts of the River Severn, and large bags of fish around 2lb were common. Since then, the Barbel has spread throughout the system, and very large specimens can be caught in the River Teme and Warwickshire Avon, as well as their more traditional locations such as the Hampshire Avon and Dorset Stour.

Baits

A favourite bait for Barbel is luncheon meat cut into cubes, but more recently pellets and boilies have become popular for the larger specimens.

Feeding the swim with boiled hempseed and then fishing a larger bait over the top is a popular method, the hempseed both attracting the barbel into the swim, and keeping them there.

Tactics

Barbel are usually caught by legering tactics.

As Barbel are perfectly adapted to living in very fast water, it is sometimes necessary to use very heavy weights to present a bait to them. In the faster reaches of rivers such as the River Severn, a heavy swimfeeder will get both the bait and some attractor feed to the fish.

Frequent casting is required to get a good quantity of loose feed into the swim in the heavy current.

In calmer swims, such as are found on the River Teme, a bed of feed such as hempseed can be laid down, and a larger bait fished over the top.

A similar stalking approach to that employed for chub can also be a successful method on smaller rivers that are known to hold Barbel.

Bleak

Latin name: Alburnus alburnus

The Bleak is a small silver fish that is mostly found in rivers.

A shoal fish, large numbers of them can be found near the surface where they will often attack baits intended for other species before it has had time to fall through the water.

Baits

Small maggot baits such as Pinkies or Squatts are a good bait for Bleak.

Tactics

Bleak are rarely the intended species of the general coarse angler, although they are sometimes targeted by match anglers as they are easy to catch and due to their large numbers can be caught in quantity to make up a match winning weight.

To catch them, use light float gear set to fish near the surface and be ready to strike as soon as you see the float or line move. Hooks should be very small, no larger than size 20 and preferably smaller.

Bream

Latin name Abramis brama (Common Bream), Blicca bjoernika (Silver Bream)

The Bream is a deep bodied fish that is relatively thin across the body. Common Bream can grow to a large size and while small bream of both species are silver in colour, large Common Bream can be a bronze colour.

Silver Bream whilst very similar in appearance do not grow so large and retain the silver colouration that they share will smaller Common Bream.

Bream are found in stillwaters such as lakes and canals and the slower reaches of rivers. A shoal fish, large catches of Bream are possible.

Baits

All maggot baits as well as worm will catch Bream of all sizes.

Larger Bream can be caught using sweetcorn, bread and the more modern Boilie and Pellet baits favoured by Carp anglers.

Tactics

Legering for bream using a groundbait feeder is a popular method for Bream fishing.

Bream have sensitive mouths, so small fine wire hooks are often used, along with very fine quivertips to indicate the least movement.

Bullhead

Latin name Cottus Gobio

Also known as the Millers Thumb, the Bullhead is a small fish with a large flattened head.

Rarely targeted by anglers, unless they are intent on getting into the record books with a particularly large specimen of the species, this greedy fish will often take maggots or quite large worms intended for other species.

Baits

Bullhead will take maggots and worms.

Tactics

Difficult to target specifically, but legering with a bunch of maggots or a worm where Bullhead are known to exist may get you into the record books for micro species!

Carp

Latin name Cyprinus carpio

The Carp is a deep bodied fish with large scales, a pair of barbels and and a dorsal fin with a large base.

Scale variations have led to the terms 'Fully Scaled Common', 'Leather Carp' and 'Mirror Carp' but all are of the same species.

Once regarded as almost impossible to catch, Carp are now the most widely caught fish in the UK, having been stocked in large numbers into commercial fisheries where they are popular with both match anglers and pleasure anglers.

Baits

On heavily stocked commercial fisheries, Carp will take most baits including maggots, bread, worms, sweetcorn and pellets.

Boilies are used to catch the larger specimens.

Tactics

Smaller Carp can be caught by most float fishing and legering techniques, as well as floating baits such as breadcrust.

Larger Carp are usually fished for with specialist leger rigs, and by stalking individual fish with float fished or free lined baits.

Catfish

Latin name Silurus glanis

The European Catfish, also knows as the Danubian Catfish and Wels is a powerful fish with a large mouth flanked by 6 barbels.

Capable of growing to a large size, the Catfish is found in only a few waters in the UK where it has been stocked in lakes, ponds and canals.

A solitary fish, Catfish are is seldom seen by Anglers unless they catch one.

Where Catfish are known to be stocked, they are more likely to be caught during the night than in daytime.

Baits

Catfish will take most baits intended for Carp and Pike.

Favourite baits are deadbaits, shrimp and squid. Fishmeal boilies have also been known to catch Catfish.

Tactics

Baits presented either on float or leger tackle will take Catfish, but the size and power of these fish dictates that the tackle must be strong.

Chub

Latin name Leuciscus cephalus

The chub has a large mouth, thick set body and dark edged scales. It lives primarily in rivers, but can also be found in some lakes and canals.

Small chub can be found in shoals while larger chub are often more solitary creatures with their own territories.

The chub is a favourite of river anglers and even very small rivers can hold quite large specimens, usually occupying the deeper pools where they make their home among the sunken roots of trees and bushes.

Baits

Chub will take almost any bait at times, including maggots and worms where there are not too many smaller fish to take the bait first, but firm favourites are bread in all its forms and cheese either used on its own or mixed with breadcrumbs to make a strongly flavoured paste.

Tactics

A roving approach is usually best for catching chub in small and medium sized rivers. A leger rig using just enough weight to hold bottom should be cast into any likely spot near bushes or trees in the deeper parts of the river.

Sensitive bite detection is rarely necessary as chub bite boldly and it pays to keep your hand on the rod when waiting for a bite.

After you have caught one, or perhaps two chub from a swim, it is time to move on. If you have a stretch of river pretty much to yourself, you can bait several swims with mashed or liquidised bread, and then fish each in turn, hopefully taking a fish or two from each as you return along the bank.

Tread carefully and try to be inconspicuous, especially on small rivers. Although chub will take a bait boldly, they are a cautious fish, and can seem to disappear into the depths if they are disturbed by an angler moving against the skyline or causing a noisy vibration on the bank.

Crucian Carp

Latin name Carassius carassius

The Crucian Carp is a deep bodied stocky fish, similar in appearance to the Common Carp, but does not grow as large.

A spirited fighter, easily recognisable by its rich golden colour, the Crucian Carp is a popular fish with Anglers, and if you connect with a shoal of them you can have a good day's sport.

Primarily a still water fish, the Crucian Carp is found in many pools and small lakes. Some rivers and canals also hold small populations.

Baits

Crucian Carp will take most baits including maggots, bread, worms, sweetcorn and pellets.

Tactics

No special tactics are required and still water float fishing and light legering techniques can be used to catch Crucian Carp.

Dace

Latin name Leuciscus leuciscus

Dace are slim silver fish that are very similar in appearance to small Chub.

Dace do not grow very large, and one of near to 1lb would be a very good specimen. What they lack in size, they make up in numbers and large shoals of them can often be seen on or near the surface of rivers in the summer months.

The Dace is widely distributed, but prefers fast flowing water so is mostly found in rivers although there are small populations of Dace in some still waters.

Baits

Dace are generally fished for with using small baits such as maggots and small pieces of bread but larger specimens can be caught using bread flak, paste and worms.

Tactics

Light float fishing methods on rivers will account for Dace where they will often be caught as part of a mixed bag with Roach.

Being primarily 'up in the water' feeders, a lightly shotted rig that allows the bait to fall slowly through the swim will usually work best, but a light swimfeeder rig fished in conjunction with a very sensitive quivertip can work on days when the fish are feeding on the bottom.

You will need quick reactions when Dace fishing as they can eject the bait very quickly and a fast strike is required.

Eel

Latin name Anguilla anguilla

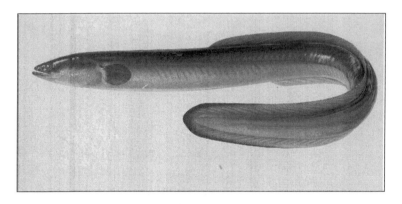

Although technically the Eel is not a fish, it is often caught by Anglers and is included in the licence for Coarse fish.

Unmistakeable because of its snake-like appearance, the Eel is widely distributed throughout British waters, but is most likely to be encountered in number in rivers and drains.

Eels can grow very large, the larger specimens occasionally being caught by Pike Anglers fishing with dead baits.

Baits

Eels will take most live baits used by Anglers such as Maggots and Worms. Larger specimens will take dead baits of whole or sectioned coarse and sea fish.

Tactics

Large Eels are usually fished for on leger tackle using deadbaits or bunches of large worms.

Grayling

Latin name Thymallus thymallus

The Grayling known as 'The lady of the stream' is a silver coloured fish with a large sail shaped dorsal fin and an additional adipose fin near the tail that is also found in game fish such as Trout.

The Grayling will generally be found in the faster parts of rivers.

As Grayling spawn at the same time as Coarse fish, they are popular with Game Anglers as they allow fly fishing methods to be used when Trout are not in season.

Baits

Grayling where present in reasonable numbers can be taken on maggots in a mixed bag of Dace and Roach, but are more often fished for by game anglers using artificial flies.

Tactics

Float fishing with maggots is a good method for catching Grayling, but they will also take legered baits.

Fly fishing is also a popular method for catching Grayling and they will take both dry (floating) and wet (sinking) flies.

There are a number of fly patterns developed especially for Grayling fishing, but they will also take flies intended for Trout.

Gudgeon

Latin name Gobio gobio

Gudgeon are a small fish that resemble small Barbel. They are present in a wide variety of waters.

Some canals have very large populations of Gudgeon, but the larger specimens are to be found in rivers where they are often caught by anglers targeting other species such as Roach and Dace.

Gudgeon feed freely and boldly, often pulling the float several inches below the surface. They are most likely to be caught down in the water, on or near the bed of the river or canal.

Baits

Maggots, especially Pinkies are a good bait for Gudgeon.

Tactics

Fishing close in with a small whip on canals is an effective method for catching gudgeon.

Small amounts of loose feed and groundbait should be fed regularly to keep the Gudgeon in the swim and feeding.

It often pays to feed two or three different lines, and switch to another when bites slow on one line. Continue feeding all lines, and over the course of a session you can catch a large number of Gudgeon.

Loach

Latin name Cobitis taenia (Spined Loach), Noemacheilus barbatulus (Stone Loach)

Two species of loach are found in British waters; the Spined Loach and the Stone Loach.

Both species have barbels, those on the spined loach being smaller. They are very small fish, rarely exceeding a few inches, and are more likely to be caught by small boys with a net, than an angler with rod and line, although the odd one may be caught when legering small baits in small rivers.

Baits

Loach will take maggots and small worms.

Tactics

Rolling up your trouser legs and using a net to catch Loach that are disturbed by moving stones on the river bed is your best bet, but if you are intent on catching every species of fish that swims using rod and line, you may be lucky if you persevere with a small maggot or a piece of a small red worm on light leger tackle where Loach are known to be present.

Minnow

Latin name Phoxinus phoxinus

The minnow is a very small fish with dark markings along the flank. It has quite a blunt snout and very small scales.

Minnows are found, sometimes in very large quantities, in lakes and rivers where they swim in large shoals.

Generally regarded as a nuisance fish when they snatch a bait intended for larger species, minnows are rarely fished for deliberately except by very small boys and anglers who require a quantity to use as live bait for perch or trout.

Baits

Almost any small bait will be taken by Minnows, several of them often racing to take a small maggot or piece of bread at the same time.

Tactics

When all else fails, a few Minnows snatched using a pinkie on a light whip rig at the end of a disappointing day can be fun, especially as in clear water they are often found in large shoals very close to the bank and larger individuals can be targeted by sight.

Perch

Latin name Perca fluviatilis

The Perch is a very distinctive fish with a large spiked Dorsal fin and striped markings.

Populations of Perch exist in most British waters. Small Perch live in shoals, whilst the largest specimens tend to be solitary.

Perch are bold voracious fish, and a small Perch is often the first fish caught by young Anglers as they are not tackle shy and bite boldly.

Baits

Small perch will take Maggots and Worms, the larger fish being caught on small fish baits, large worms and artificial spinning baits.

Tactics

Small Perch can be taken on most float fishing and legering methods where they will often make up part of a mixed bag.

Where large Perch are known to be present they can be caught using small artificial spinners.

Legering with large worms such as Lobs and Dendrobaenas is a also a good technique that can account for some quite sizable Perch.

Pike

Latin name Esox lucius

The Pike is a predatory fish that can grow to a very large size. It is a long fish, built for bursts of speed, and with a mouth full of sharp teeth for seizing its prey.

Well camouflaged in bands of dark and light green or black, it is able to lurk unseen among reeds and other plants from which it can emerge vary quickly to seize prey fish that pass by.

Baits

Small Pike will take maggots and worms, but the larger specimens are caught using live and dead fish baits as well as artificial lures such as Spinners, Spoons, Plugs and the more recent Jelly Baits.

Tactics

Pike will generally be found where there is cover that will hide them from their prey.

A lure will often work well if pulled through the water near lily pads and reeds.

Most lures are capable of catching Pike and often a single fish can be targeted if sighted.

Pike will often emerge from underwater vegetation to follow a lure, and it often pays to speed up the rate of retrieve when this happens to goad the Pike into taking what appears to be a prey fish trying to escape.

Live baits, where allowed, will account for Pike either fished under a heavy float and allowed to swim freely, or on a Paternoster float-leger rig. Most coarse fish are suitable as live bait, but the practice is not always allowed.

Where live baiting is not permitted, Pike can also be taken on dead baits, including sea fish such as Mackerel, Sprats and Herring. These can be fished either on a Paternoster float rig or leger rig.

Roach

Latin name Rutilus Rutilus

The Roach is a silver fish with red fins, present in most British coarse fishing waters.

Most coarse anglers will have caught a roach early in their fishing career as they are a free feeding shoal fish that will take most small baits.

Baits

Roach are generally fished for with maggots, bread flake or paste being a popular bait for the larger specimens. They will also take worms, pellets and small boilies.

Tactics

Most coarse fishing tactics will catch roach depending on the type of water and conditions.

In rivers they can be fished for with light tackle by trotting a stick float with the stream, using maggots as the bait and ensuring a steady stream of free offerings are thrown in to keep the roach in the swim and competing for food.

Larger river specimens can be taken using a leger or swimfeeder rig, with larger baits such as worm, bread flake or paste allowing selective targeting of the larger specimens.

In ponds, lakes and canals, pole or whip tactics can account for large bags of small or medium sized roach using pinkies or maggots with a cloud groundbait.

Rudd

Latin name Scardinius erythrophthalmus

The Rudd is a similar fish to the Roach, but is often a more golden colour and slightly deeper in the body. While less common than the Roach, the Rudd is widely distributed throughout british stillwater coarse fisheries such as ponds, lakes and canals as well as slow moving rivers.

In waters where Roach and Rudd exist together they will often be taken in a mixed bag, the rudd often feeding higher in the water than Roach and taking baits on or near the surface.

Baits

Like Roach, Rudd are generally fished for with maggots, with bread flake or paste being a popular bait for the larger specimens. They will also take worms, pellets and small boilies.

Tactics

In addition to float and leger tactics, Rudd can be taken by presenting floating breadflake, and they will also take an artificial fly presented with fly tackle.

Like the roach, floatfished or legered breadflake can account for the larger specimens where they are present.

In ponds, lakes and canals, pole or whip tactics can account for large bags of small or medium sized Rudd using pinkies or maggots with a cloud groundbait.

Ruffe

Latin name Gymnocephalus cernua

The Ruffe is similar in appearance to the Perch, but with a drab colouring in comparison to the bold stripes of the Perch.

Ruffe do not grow to a large size, and although they are quite widespread they do not exist in large numbers and are not regularly encountered by most Anglers.

Baits

Maggots and small worms will catch Ruffe.

Tactics

Ruffe are not usually deliberately targeted by Anglers but where they are present they will be taken by most float fishing and legering methods while fishing for a mixed bag.

Stickleback

Latin name Gasterosteus aculeatus (Three Spined Stickleback), Pungitius pungitius (Ten Spined Stickleback)

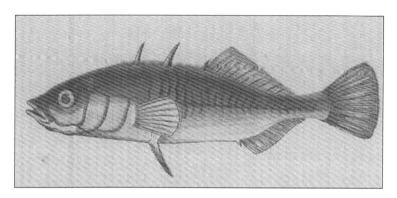

Easily recognisable, and possibly the best known British freshwater fish, these fish have three or ten spines along the back before the dorsal fin.

Of the two, the three spined stickleback is the most common and is found everywhere from small ditches to rivers and lakes. The ten spined stickleback is more rare, and is found in stagnant waters in mud and weed.

Baits

Sticklebacks will take maggots and worms.

Tactics

Whilst not a fish you would deliberately target, you may get one when using a small worm as bait.

If the worm is only hooked once in the middle of the body, you may even get two at once, one on each end as they are not often hooked, but can suck in quite a large length of a thin red worm or brandling and will remain attached after you lift your tackle out of the water.

Tench

Latin name Tinca tinca

The Tench is a thick set fish with a distinctive olive green or brown colouring. A large tail fin is a feature of this species which allows it to swim strongly. Tench will often be found in the margin areas among lily pads and thick weed.

A popular fish with Anglers primarily in the summer months, Tench are widespread thoughout british waters, but most likely to be encountered in lakes, ponds, slow flowing rivers and some canals.

Baits

Most baits will take tench, popular baits being Maggots, worms, sweetcorn, bread and small boilies.

Tactics

Tench are bottom feeding fish, so float tackle set to present the bait on the bottom is a popular and succesful method.

Tench bites are rarely bold and fast and knowing when to strike can be difficult for inexperienced Anglers. Sometimes it is necessary to wait for this positive indication, on other days an earlier strike is needed.

Tench can also be caught using leger tactics, and are often caught by Anglers targeting Carp.

Zander

Latin name Stizostedion lucioperca

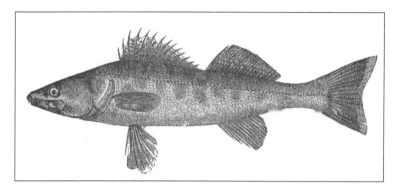

The Zander is a powerful predator that can grow to a large size. The Zander is sometimes referred to as a Pike-Perch due to its similarities with both fish but it is a separate species.

Whilst not as widely distributed as either the Pike or the Perch, large populations exist in some rivers and canals.

Baits

Zander are generally fished for using live and dead fish baits as well as artificial lures such as Spinners, Spoons, Plugs and the more recent Jelly Baits.

Tactics

Live baits, where allowed, will account for Zander either fished under a heavy float and allowed to swim freely, or on a Paternoster float-leger rig. Most coarse fish are suitable as live bait, but the practice is not always allowed.

Where live baiting is not permitted, Zander can also be taken on dead baits, including sea fish such as Mackerel, Sprats and Herring. These can be fished either on a Paternoster float rig or leger rig.

Zander can also be caught on a variety of artificial spinning baits.

ABOUT THE AUTHOR

As someone who was born in the middle part of the last century, before video games, colour television and the many other electronic distractions of today I have fond memories of the time that I spent reading old fishing books, making fishing tackle, and learning to catch fish in the local stream.

There were few 'commercial fisheries' then. Waters were, by and large, in a natural state and not stocked to the brim with artificially reared carp of uniform size that will compete for any food thrown at them. In fact, Carp were considered the most difficult fish to catch, whereas today if you want to catch a fish of more than a few ounces, its probably easier to catch a carp than anything else.

When deciding to write this guide, my aim was to provide an introduction to coarse fishing that would allow a beginner to the sport to experience some of the 'magic' that I remember from my youth. Coarse fishing, or angling, is not, to me at least, just about who can catch the most or the biggest fish. It's about learning a craft and developing an appreciation for fish and their surroundings.

I get as much pleasure, maybe more, from catching a few small fish from a tiny unspoilt river, as from 'bagging up' on a well stocked artificial pond. Coarse fishing, if practiced in a more traditional way, has infinite variety, and success is not measured by the number or size of fish caught alone.

Paul Duffield

2771223R00047

Printed in Great Britain
by Amazon.co.uk, Ltd.,
Marston Gate.